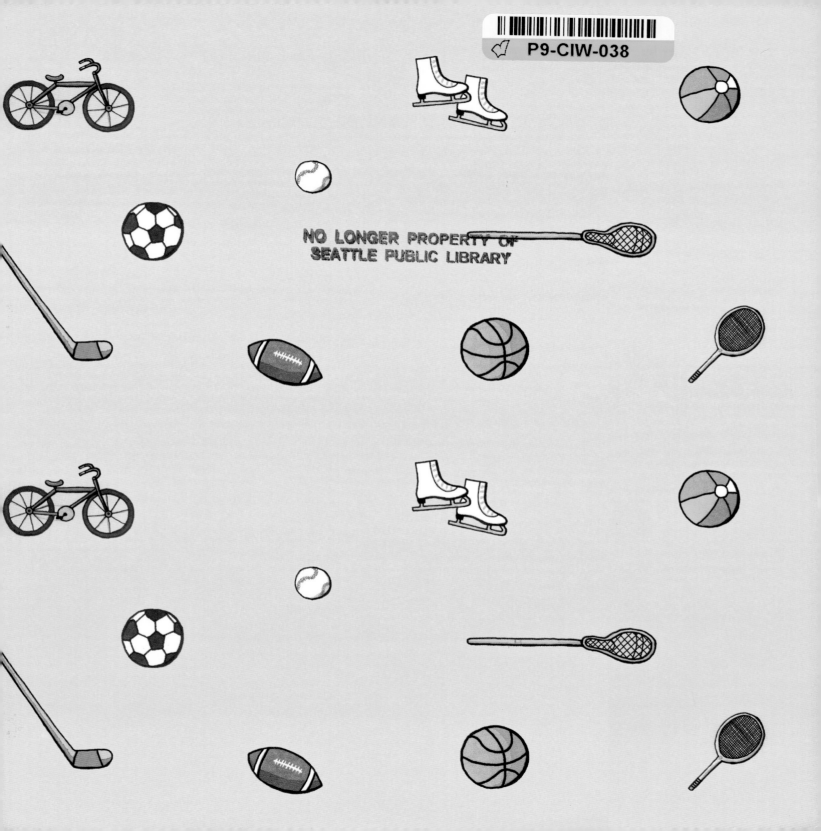

For John, Phil, and Rob

Henry Holt and Company, *Publishers since 1866*
Henry Holt® is a registered trademark of Macmillan Publishing Group, LLC
175 Fifth Avenue, New York, NY 10010 · mackids.com

Library of Congress Control Number: 2018935734
ISBN 978-1-62779-349-0

Our books may be purchased in bulk for promotional, educational, or business use. Please contact your local
bookseller or the Macmillan Corporate and Premium Sales Department at (800) 221-7945 ext. 5442
or by e-mail at MacmillanSpecialMarkets@macmillan.com.

First edition, 2019 / Designed by April Ward and Sophie Erb
The artist used watercolor, pen, and ink on Fabriano watercolor paper.
Printed in China by RR Donnelley Asia Printing Solutions Ltd., Dongguan City, Guangdong Province

1   3   5   7   9   10   8   6   4   2

Leo Landry

HOME RUN, TOUCHDOWN, BASKET, GOAL!

Sports Poems for Little Athletes

GODWINBOOKS

Henry Holt and Company
New York

Up!

I chalk my hands and look right at
The members of my team.
A simple vault and up I leap
Onto the balance beam.

An arabesque, a pivot turn,
My handstand is outstanding.
Just one more move and off I go.
Hooray I've stuck the landing!

Teammates

I scoop the ball into my stick
And pass it to my teammate—quick!
He takes a shot and misses, then
The ball rebounds to me again.
Another try (I'm not done yet) . . .
The ball sails right into the net!

For Kicks

We meet at the dojo
Each Saturday at ten.
We bow and thank our sensei;
We bow and we begin.
I challenge you upon the mat.
You raise a single hand.
I jump and then I throw a kick—
I roll and then I stand!

Wheels

I strap my helmet on my head
And settle on the seat.
My handlebars will steer me straight
And soon I'll cruise the street.

I shift and pedal, shift again.
My wheels are turning fast.
Around a curve, and then a sprint—
I've won the race at last!

Ice Time

My skates are laced.
I've got my stick.
The ice is very cold and slick.

The goalie stands
Inside the net.
He wants to block my shot I bet.

I pass the puck.
You pass it back.
We move it down the ice on track.

I skate so fast,
I'm on a roll.
I take a shot and holler,
GOAL!

Swish!

I dribble,
I run fast down court,
Although my legs are very short.

The net is high,
I take a shot—
The ball goes off the rim a lot.

You get the rebound,
Pass the ball.
The game is on the line—that's all!

I bounce the ball and make a wish.
I take the shot, it falls in—
SWISH!

Cannonball!

We learned to swim the other day,
It wasn't hard at all.
The doggie-paddle, frog kick,
Then the breaststroke and the crawl.

The butterfly and sidestroke,
And yet that wasn't all—
All together, 1, 2, 3,
Let's do a

Cannonball!

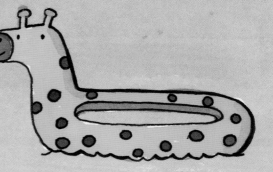

Go Long!

My pads are on,
My helmet tight,
It's kickoff at the game tonight.

Hike one, hike two,
I drop back fast.
I want to throw a forward pass.

Go long! I shout.
You get the hint.
You're headed for the end zone—*sprint!*

I throw the ball.
You turn around.
I raise my arms and yell,

TOUCHDOWN!

Tennis, Anyone?

You toss the ball into the air,
I'm waiting for your serve.
The tennis ball comes at me fast,
I've almost lost my nerve.

It bounces once, I take a swing.
The ball is high above.
You've served another ace again—
The score is forty-love!

Brrr!

I love to glide upon the ice
And dance upon my skates,
From axels, quads, and spirals
To amazing figure-eights.

I dream about a perfect "10"
And taking home the gold,
But now I want my sweater
For I'm getting rather cold!

Soccer Match

I've got my ball,
I'm set to play,
I'm ready for the match today.

I kick the ball.
You use your head.
The ball comes back to me instead.

I dribble down the field, and then
I pass the ball to you again.

You kick once more.
I see a hole.
The ball sneaks by, we cry out,
GOAL!

Play Ball!

I've got my ball,
I've got my glove,
I'm ready for the game I love.

I've got my cleats,
I've got my bat,
And don't forget my baseball hat.

I throw a pitch,
You take a swing.
The ball sails over everything.

You run the bases one by one.
We gather 'round and shout,

HOME RUN!